* Non Profit Organization
** Referral Service
*** Private Attorney

List of Pro Bono Legal Service Providers

Updated January 2017

http://www.justice.gov/eoir/list-pro-bono-legal-service-providers

Table of Contents

I0502414

ARIZONA

List of Pro Bono Legal Service Providers

Updated January 2017

http://www.justice.gov/eoir/list-pro-bono-legal-service-providers

Eloy Immigration Court

Eloy, Arizona

Florence Immigrant and Refugee Rights Project*

P.O. Box 654
Florence, AZ 85232
Phone: (520) 868-0191
firrp@firrp.org
firrp.org
• All aspects of removal defense for ICE detainees

List of Pro Bono Legal Service Providers

Updated January 2017

http://www.justice.gov/eoir/list-pro-bono-legal-service-providers

Phoenix Immigration Court

Phoenix, Arizona
Florence Immigrant and Refugee Rights Project* P.O. Box 654 Florence, AZ 85232 Phone: (602) 307-1008 kids@firrp.org firrp.org • Children only: asylum, SIJS, T and U visas • No walk-ins, please call to make an appointment

List of Pro Bono Legal Service Providers

Updated January 2017

http://www.justice.gov/eoir/list-pro-bono-legal-service-providers

Florence Immigration Court

Florence, Arizona

Florence Immigrant and Refugee Rights Project*

P.O. Box 654
Florence, AZ 85232
Phone: (520) 868-0191
firrp@firrp.org
firrp.org
- All aspects of removal defense for ICE detainees

List of Pro Bono Legal Service Providers

http://www.justice.gov/eoir/list-pro-bono-legal-service-providers

Tucson Immigration Court

Tucson, Arizona	
Immigration Law Clinic* University of Arizona Rogers College of Law 1145 N. Mountain Ave. Tucson, AZ 85719 Tel: (520) 626-5232 • Provides free consultations and assistance • Appointments in Sept., Oct., Nov., Feb., March, and April only	**Florence Immigrant and Refugee Rights Project*** P.O. Box 654 Florence, AZ 85232 Phone: (520) 203-7912 kids@firrp.org firrp.org • Children only: asylum, SIJS, T and U visas • No walk-ins, please call to make an appointment

CALIFORNIA

* Non Profit Organization
** Referral Service
*** Private Attorney

List of Pro Bono Legal Service Providers

Updated January 2017

http://www.justice.gov/eoir/list-pro-bono-legal-service-providers

Adelanto Immigration Court

Adelanto, California	
Esperanza Immigrant Rights Project* Catholic Charities of Los Angeles 1530 James M Wood Blvd Los Angeles, CA 90015 Phone: (213) 251-3505 Fax: (213) 487-0986 esperanza-la.org • Mon-Fri 8:30am-5:30pm • Serving counties of Los Angeles, Orange, Riverside, San Bernardino, Ventura, Kern, & Santa Barbara • Assist in various forms of immigration relief, victims of crime • Reduced fee, nominal fee, or pro bono depending on need and grant availability Languages: Spanish or interpeter services	**El Rescate*** 1501 West 8th St. Suite 100 Los Angeles, CA 90017 (213) 387-3284 • Bond hearings • Removal proceedings • ICE paroled request

List of Pro Bono Legal Service Providers

Updated January 2017

http://www.justice.gov/eoir/list-pro-bono-legal-service-providers

Imperial Immigration Court

Imperial and El Centro, California

El Rescate*

1501 West 8th St. Suite 100
Los Angeles, CA 90017
(213) 387-3284
• Bond hearings
• Removal proceedings
• ICE paroled request

List of Pro Bono Legal Service Providers

http://www.justice.gov/eoir/list-pro-bono-legal-service-providers

Los Angeles Immigration Court

Los Angeles, California (page 1 of 2)	
Kids In Need of Defense (KIND)* Los Angeles City Office c/o Chadbourne & Parke LLP 350 South Grand Ave., 32nd Floor Los Angeles, CA 90071 Tel: (213) 892-2043 Fax: (213) 892-2054 infolosangeles@supportkind.org supportkind.org • KIND only represents minors and unnacompanied children • KIND ayuda a menores de edad y nino/as no-acompanados	**Public Counsel*** 610 South Ardmore Avenue Los Angeles, CA 90005 Tel: (213) 385-2977 ext 600 www.publiccounsel.org • Resources permitting, we will provide pro bono representation to asylum seekers, victims of crime including domestic violence and human trafficking.
Immigrant Defenders Law Center* 634 S. Spring St, 10th floor Los Angeles, CA 90014 Phone: (213) 634-0999 Fax: (213) 634-0999 info@immdef.org immdef.org • Unaccompanied minors only • Languages: Spanish	**International Institute of Los Angeles*** 3845 Selig Place Los Angeles, CA 90031 (323) 264-6217 or 14701 Friar St. Van Nuys, CA 91411 (818) 988-1332 or 1333 • Will not represent criminals. • May charge nominal fee. • Will represent alien in asylum.
Esperanza Immigrant Rights Project* Catholic Charities of Los Angeles 1530 James M Wood Blvd Los Angeles, CA 90015 Phone: (213) 251-3505 Fax: (213) 487-0986 esperanza-la.org • Mon-Fri 8:30am-5:30pm • Serving counties of Los Angeles, Orange, Riverside, San Bernardino, Ventura, Kern, & Santa Barbara • Assist in various forms of immigration relief, victims of crime • Reduced fee, nominal fee, or pro bono depending on need and grant availability • Languages: Spanish or interpeter services	**El Rescate*** 1501 West 8th St. Suite 100 Los Angeles, CA 90017 (213) 387-3284 • Removal proceedings and bond hearings

List of Pro Bono Legal Service Providers

Updated January 2017

http://www.justice.gov/eoir/list-pro-bono-legal-service-providers

Los Angeles, California (page 2 of 2)

Roberto K. Amaya, Esq.*	**Akram Abusharar, Esq.***
Law Offices of Roberto K. Amaya 1672 West Ave. J, Suite 207 Lancaster, CA 93534 Tel: (661) 916-7801 and 14500 Roscoe Blvd., Suite 400 Panorama City, CA 91402 Tel: (661) 916-7801	501 N. Brookhurst St., Suite #202 Anaheim, CA 92801 Tel: (714) 535-5600 Fax: (714) 535-5605

List of Pro Bono Legal Service Providers

Updated January 2017

http://www.justice.gov/eoir/list-pro-bono-legal-service-providers

Otay Mesa Immigration Court

Otay Mesa Detention Center, San Diego, California	
Casa Cornelia Law Center* 2760 Fifth Avenue, Suite 200 San Diego, CA 92103 Tel: (619) 231-7788 Fax: (619) 231-7784 LawCenter@CasaCornelia.org casacornelia.org • Asylum, victims of serious crime	**El Rescate*** 1501 West 8th St. Suite 100 Los Angeles, CA 90017 (213) 387-3284 • Bond hearings • Removal proceedings • ICE paroled request

* Non Profit Organization
** Referral Service
*** Private Attorney

List of Pro Bono Legal Service Providers

Updated January 2017

http://www.justice.gov/eoir/list-pro-bono-legal-service-providers

San Diego Immigration Court

San Diego, California	
ABA Immigration Justice Project* 2727 Camino del Rio South, Suite 223 San Diego, CA 92108 (619) 655-8817 • Refer limited detained and non-detained cases to Pro Bono Attorneys • Offer legal orientations to individuals in removal proceedings at the San Diego Immigration Court, Wednesdays 8:30 am - 10:00 am (English and Espanol). Call for more information.	**Casa Cornelia Law Center*** 2760 Fifth Avenue, Suite 200 San Diego, CA 92103 Tel: (619) 231-7788 Fax: (619) 231-7784 LawCenter@CasaCornelia.org casacornelia.org • Asylum, unaccompanied minors, victims of serious crime
Legal Aid Society of San Diego* 110 South Euclid Ave. San Diego, CA 92114 1-877 Legal Aid (877-534-2524), Toll Free • No charge. • Will not represent asylum cases.	**Ali Golchin, Esq.***** Golchin and Associates 1251 Third Ave., Ste. 203 Chula Vista, Ca 91911 Tel: (619) 325-7555 • Will not represent aliens in asylum cases. • Representation limited to the San Diego district
Mari Kleven, Esq.*** 964 Fifth Avenue, Suite 214 San Diego, CA 92101 marikleven@gmail.com Tel: 619-752-4646 Fax: 619-564-7717	

List of Pro Bono Legal Service Providers

Updated January 2017

http://www.justice.gov/eoir/list-pro-bono-legal-service-providers

San Francisco Immigration Court

San Francisco, California (page 1 of 2)	
Asian Law Caucus* 55 Columbus Ave. San Francisco, CA 94111 (415) 896-1701 (415) 896-1702 advancingjustice-alc.org • Specialize in criminal removal defense • Rarely take asylum cases • Languages: Mandarin, Cantonese, Vietnamese, Hindi	**Immigration Law Clinic** **U.C. Davis School of Law*** One Shields Ave TB 30 Davis, CA 95616-5201 (530) 752-6942 • Holly Cooper, Associate Director and Amagda Perez, Staff Attorney • Serving Northern and Central California • Detained and non-detained cases • Mon-Fri, 9am-5pm • Languages: Spanish, Italian
Asian Pacific Island Legal Outreach* 1121 Mission Street San Francisco, CA 94103 (415) 567-6255 • Willing to represent indigent aliens in asylum proceedings Languages: Cantonese, Japanese, Korean, Mandarin, and Vietnamese	**La Raza Centro Legal*** 474 Valencia St., Ste. 295 San Francisco, CA 94103 Phone: (415) 575-3500 Fax: (415) 255-7593 lrcl.org • Non-detained only • Languages: Spanish
Asylum Program of the San Francisco Lawyers' Committee for Civil Rights* 131 Steuart Street, Ste. 400 San Francisco, CA 94105 (415) 543-9697, ext. 202 • Contact Tel: Silvia Contreras Mon.-Fri. 9 am - 5:30 pm • Pro Bono or nominal fee • Must meet income guidelines • Interviews Wed-Fri by appt • Languages: Spanish & French • Serves San Francisco Bay area • Asylum cases screened for finances and meritorious claims	**Social Justice Collaborative*** 420 3rd Street, Suite 130 Oakland, CA 94607 Tel: (510) 992-3964 Fax: (510) 255-5200 office@socialjusticecollaborative.org www.socialjusticecollaborative.org • Consultations by Appointment Only • Languages – Spanish, Tamil • Deportation defense priority

* Non Profit Organization
** Referral Service
*** Private Attorney

List of Pro Bono Legal Service Providers

Updated January 2017

http://www.justice.gov/eoir/list-pro-bono-legal-service-providers

San Francisco, California (page 2 of 2)	
Community Legal Services in East Palo Alto (CLSEPA)* 2117-B University Avenue East Palo Alto, CA 94303 Tel: (650) 326-6440 Fax: (866) 688-5204 immigration@clsepa.org clsepa.org • Residents of San Mateo and Santa Clara counties only • No collect calls • Languages: Spanish	**National Center for Lesbian Rights (NCLR)*** 870 Market St., Ste. 370 San Francisco, CA 94102 Tel: (415) 392-6257 Fax: (415) 392-8442 • Seeks to represent lesbian, gay, bisexual, and transgender (LGBT) indigent aliens in asylum proceedings • Assists LGBT aliens and immigrants in understanding visas, asylum claims, and HIV exclusion, and provides legal and practical strategies for bi-national couples
Kids in Need of Defense (KIND)* San Francisco Office 200 Pine St, 3rd floor San Francisco, CA 94104 Tel: (415) 694-7389 Fax: (415) 956-9022 infosanfrancisco@supportkind.org supportkind.org • KIND only represents minors and unnacompanied children • KIND ayuda a menores de edad y nino/as no-acompanados	**Centro Legal de la Raza*** 3400 E. 12th Street Oakland, CA 94601 Tel: (510) 437-1554 Fax: (510) 437-9164 www.centrolegal.org

* Non Profit Organization
** Referral Service
*** Private Attorney

List of Pro Bono Legal Service Providers

Updated January 2017

http://www.justice.gov/eoir/list-pro-bono-legal-service-providers

COLORADO

List of Pro Bono Legal Service Providers

http://www.justice.gov/eoir/list-pro-bono-legal-service-providers

Aurora Immigration Court

Aurora, Colorado

Catholic Charities* 2500 1st Ave., Bldg. CB Greeley, CO 80631 (970) 353-6433	**Catholic Immigration Services Catholic Charities*** 4045 Pecos Street Denver, CO 80211 (303) 742-4971
Catholic Charities* 1004 Grand Ave. Glenwood Springs, CO 81601 (970) 384-2060	• May charge a nominal fee. • Will represent aliens in asylum. No collect calls.
	Rocky Mountain Immigrant Advocacy Network (RMAIN)* 3489 W. 72nd St, Suite 211 Westminster, CO 80030 Tel: (303) 433-2812 Fax: (303) 344-32823 rmain.org • Individuals in immigration detention • Children's immigration matters

List of Pro Bono Legal Service Providers

http://www.justice.gov/eoir/list-pro-bono-legal-service-providers

Denver Immigration Court

Denver, Colorado

Catholic Charities* 2500 1st Ave., Bldg. CB Greeley, CO 80631 (970) 353-6433	**Catholic Immigration Services Catholic Charities*** 4045 Pecos Street Denver, CO 80211 (303) 742-4971
Catholic Charities* 1004 Grand Ave. Glenwood Springs, CO 81601 (970) 384-2060	• May charge a nominal fee. • Will represent aliens in asylum. No collect calls.
	Rocky Mountain Immigrant Advocacy Network (RMAIN)* 3489 W. 72nd St, Suite 211 Westminster, CO 80030 Tel: (303) 433-2812 Fax: (303) 344-32823 rmain.org • Individuals in immigration detention • Children's immigration matters

CONNECTICUT

List of Pro Bono Legal Service Providers

Updated January 2017

http://www.justice.gov/eoir/list-pro-bono-legal-service-providers

Hartford Immigration Court

Hartford, Connecticut	
International Institute of Connecticut* (Main Office) 670 Clinton Avenue Bridgeport, CT 06605 1-888-342-2678 • Represents aliens in removal proceedings. • Represents aliens in asylum proceedings. • May consider representing aliens in detention and criminal aliens. • Provides counseling • Represents aliens in citizenship applications, green card processing, extension of visas, work authorization, and petitions for relatives.	**International Institute of Connecticut*** (Stamford Division) 34 Woodland Avenue (NEON Building) Stamford, CT 06902 Tel: (203) 965-7190 Fax: (203) 425-8927 • Represents aliens in citizenship applications, green card processing, extension of visas, work authorization, petitions for relatives. • Provides counseling.
	International Institute of Connecticut* (Hartford Division) 175 Main Street Hartford, CT 06106 (860) 692-3085 • Represents aliens in removal proceedings through Court Representation Project (cases are assigned to volunteer attorneys). • May consider representing aliens in detention and criminal aliens. • Represents aliens in asylum proceedings. • Represents aliens in citizenship applications, green card processing, extension of visas, work authorization, and petitions for relatives. • Provides counseling. • Nominal fees charged for representation. • Limited representation available from June to August.

* Non Profit Organization
** Referral Service
*** Private Attorney

List of Pro Bono Legal Service Providers

Updated January 2017

http://www.justice.gov/eoir/list-pro-bono-legal-service-providers

FLORIDA

List of Pro Bono Legal Service Providers

Updated January 2017

http://www.justice.gov/eoir/list-pro-bono-legal-service-providers

Krome Immigration Court

Krome North Processing Center, Miami, Florida

Catholic Charities Legal Services Archdiocese of Miami, Inc.* Campus of St. Stephen Catholic Church 6081 SW 21st Street Miramar, Florida 33023 Tel: (954) 486-2070 Fax: (954) 486-5090 info@cclsmiami.org cclsmiami.org • Asylum proceedings • LPR with criminal convictions • Children's cases • VAWA, T & U Visas R visas • Languages: Spanish, Haitian Creole, French	**Catholic Charities Legal Services Archdiocese of Miami, Inc.*** 7855 NW 12th Street, Suite 114 Miami, Florida 33126 Tel: (305) 887-8333 Fax: (305) 541-2741 info@cclsmiami.org cclsmiami.org • All types of cases accepted • Will be represented by main office • Will process Cuban adjustment, employment autorization, parole requests, and citizenship applications for Miami-Dade and Monroe County residents • Languages: English, Spanish

List of Pro Bono Legal Service Providers

Updated January 2017

http://www.justice.gov/eoir/list-pro-bono-legal-service-providers

Miami Immigration Court

Miami, Florida (page 1 of 2)	
Center for Immigrant Advancement, Inc. (CIMA)* 809 SW 8th St., Suite 212 Miami, FL 33130 Tel: (786) 346-3828 Fax: (305) 285-2333 • Spanish Spoken	**Americans for Immigrant Justice*** 3000 Biscayne Blvd., Ste. 400 Miami, FL 33137 (305) 573-1106 • Spanish, Creole and French spoken. • Will take Asylum cases.
American Friends Service Committee* 1175 NE 125th St, Suite 417 North Miami, FL 33161 Phone: (305) 600-5441 Fax: (305) 432-4476 lperez-renozo@afsc.org afsc.org	**Catholic Charities Legal Services Archdiocese of Miami, Inc.*** Courthouse Plaza Building 28 West Flagler Street, 10th Floor Miami, Florida 33130 Tel: (305) 373-1073 Fax: (305) 373-1173 info@cclsmiami.org http://www.cclsmiami.org
Orlando Center for Justice* 1802 N Alafaya Trail, Suite 173 Orlando, FL 32826 Tel: (407) 279-1802 info@orlandojustice.org orlandojustice.org • Languages: Spanish, Portuguese	• Representation limited to Miami Immigration Court and Krome Detention Center • Representation to residents of Monroe, Miami-Dade, and Broward Counties • All types of cases accepted • Languages: English, Spanish, Haitian-Creole, Frnach, Mandarin, other languages arranged

* Non Profit Organization
** Referral Service
*** Private Attorney

List of Pro Bono Legal Service Providers

Updated January 2017

http://www.justice.gov/eoir/list-pro-bono-legal-service-providers

Miami, Florida (page 2 of 2)

Catholic Charities Legal Services Archdiocese of Miami, Inc.*	Catholic Charities Legal Services Archdiocese of Miami, Inc.*
7855 NW 12th Street, Suite 114 Miami, Florida 33126 Tel: (305) 887-8333 Fax: (305) 541-2741 info@cclsmiami.org cclsmiami.org • All types of cases accepted • Will be represented by main office • Will process Cuban adjustment, employment autorization, parole requests, and citizenship applications for Miami-Dade and Monroe County residents • Languages: Spanish, other languages arranged	Campus of St. Stephen Catholic Church 6081 SW 21st Street Miramar, Florida 33023 Tel: (954) 486-2070 Fax: (954) 486-5090 info@cclsmiami.org cclsmiami.org • All types of cases accepted • VAWA, T & U Visas R visas • Children's cases • Representation limited to residents of Broward, Miami-Dade and Monroe Counties • Representation limited to Miami Immigration Court and Krome Detention Center • LPR with criminal convictions • Languages: Spanish, Haitian Creole, French, Mandarin, other languages arranged
Catholic Charities Legal Services Archdiocese of Palm Beach, Inc.* 100 West 20th Street Riviera Beach, FL 33404 Tel: (561) 345-2003 Fax: (561) 202-2310 & 1300 East 10th St Stuart, FL 34995 (772) 463-0445 (772) 872-0311, Fax • Representation limited to Miami Immigration Court and residents of Palm Beach, Martin, St. Lucie, Okeechobee and Indian River Counties • Asylum cases will be accepted and represented by the Palm Beach offices • Spanish spoken	**Lutheran Services Florida, Inc.*** Employability Status Assistance Refugee Legal Services 7901 4th Street North, Suite 308 St. Petersburg, Florida 33702-4313 Tel: (727) 563-9400 Fax: (727) 563-0303 • Representation limited to Orlando Immigration Court • Qualification is based on income and length of time in US. • Representation is for residents of Pinellas, Manatee, Sarasota, Desoto, East Hillsborough, Highlands, and Hardee counties. • Languages: Burmese, Bosnian, Arabic, Haitian, Creole, Spanish, French and English.

List of Pro Bono Legal Service Providers

Updated January 2017

http://www.justice.gov/eoir/list-pro-bono-legal-service-providers

Orlando Immigration Court

Orlando, Florida

Gulf Coast Legal Services, Inc.

641 First Street South
St. Petersburg, FL 33701
Tel: (727) 821-0726
Tel: 1-800-230-5920 (Toll free)
Fax: (727) 821-3340
www.gulfcoastlegal.org

• Free civil legal services to eligible clients.
• Must be income eligible.
• Must reside in Pinellas, Pasco, Manatee, Sarasota or Hillsborough Counties.

• By appointment or phone.
• Will represent aliens in asylum cases.

• Spanish spoken, other languages arranged.

• Immigration matters include asylum/VAWA cancellation/U status/trafficking victims/juveniles

Lutheran Services Florida, Inc.*
Employability Status Assistance
Refugee Legal Services
6440 Ridge Road
Port Richey, FL 34668-6748
Fax: (727) 842-4007
and
8532 SW 8th St #270
Miami, FL 33144

• Representation limited to Orlando Immigration Court
• Accept Refugees - all nationalities
• Qualification is also based on income and length of time in US.

• Representation is for residents of Pasco, Polk, North Hillsborough, Highlands and Hardee counties.
• Languages: Burmese, Bosnian, Arabic, Haitian, Creole, Spanish, French and English.

Lutheran Services Florida, Inc.*

Employability Status Assistance
Refugee Legal Services
3625 West Waters Avenue
Tampa, FL 33614-2783
Tel: (813) 877-9303
Fax: (813) 877-3813

• Representation limited to Orlando Immigration Court
• Accept Refugees - all nationalities
• Qualification is also based on income and length of time in US.

• Representation is for residents of Hillsborough, Polk, Highlands, Manatee, and Hardee.

• Languages: Burmese, Bosnian, Arabic, Haitian, Creole, Spanish, French and English.

Orlando Center for Justice*

1802 N Alafaya Trail, Suite 173
Orlando, FL 32826
(407) 279-1802
info@orlandojustice.org
orlandojustice.org
• Languages: Spanish, Portuguese

Florida Coastal School of Law*

8787 Baypine Road, Suite 255
Jacksonville, FL 32256
(904) 680-7782

Louis Gvzmann, Esq.***

Law Offices of Louis Gvzmann, Esq.
P.O. Box 390964
Deltona, Florida 32739
(386) 717-6468
• Orlando court cases only
• Languages: Spanish, Castilan, German

List of Pro Bono Legal Service Providers

http://www.justice.gov/eoir/list-pro-bono-legal-service-providers

GEORGIA

List of Pro Bono Legal Service Providers

Updated January 2017

http://www.justice.gov/eoir/list-pro-bono-legal-service-providers

Atlanta Immigration Court

Atlanta, Georgia	
Catholic Charities Atlanta* 2305 Parklake Drive, Suite 150 Building 9 Atlanta, GA 30345 (678)-222-3920 • Intake for new clients is done by telephone between 8 a.m. and 12 noon, Monday to Friday. Call (678)-222-3920. • Will not take cases involving drugs, aggravated felonies, fraud, or persons convicted of spouse or child abuse or child neglect. • Will charge nominal fee except for no fee for the homeless, detained, juvenile, and VAWA clients only. • Small consultation fee, other services are billed on a sliding scale. • Will not take cases that are best resolved by a designated school officer. • Unable to take cases from North Carolina.	**The Latin American Association (LAA)*** 2750 Buford Highway Atlanta, GA 30324 Tel: 404-471-1889 Fax: 404-389-0472 www.thelaa.org
	Access to Law Foundation* 2415 Beaver Ruin Road, Ste. B Norcross, GA 30071 Tel: (770) 685-1499 Fax: 1-888-308-1931 P.O. Box 1614, Norcross, GA 30091 www.accesstolawfoundation.org • Will represent indigent aliens in asylum proceedings • Will provide free legal services to indigent aliens • Will represent indigent aliens in asylum proceedings
North Carolina Justice and Community Development Center* Immigrants Legal Assistance Project 224 S. Dawson Street Raleigh, NC 27611 1-888-251-2776 http://www.ncjustice.org/ilap Attorneys: Attracta Kelly and Jeff Summerlin-Long Paralegal: Cristin Ruggle • Will represent asylum seekers. • Languages: Spanish • New clients accepted only on Tuesdays, must call FIRST between 9 a.m. and 5 p.m. • No walk-in clients.	• Monday to Friday 9:am to 5:00 pm • By appointment only call (770) 685-1499 All types of immigration cases including SIJS and family court proceedings • Multilingual-Spanish, French, Hindi, Urdu
	Kids in Need of Defense (KIND)* Atlanta Office 600 Peachtree St NE, Suite 5200 Atlanta, GA 30308 Tel: (404)885-3629 Fax: (404) 885-3900 infoatlanta@supportkind.org supportkind.org • KIND only represents minors and unnacompanied children • KIND ayuda a menores de edad y nino/as no-acompanados

List of Pro Bono Legal Service Providers

http://www.justice.gov/eoir/list-pro-bono-legal-service-providers

Illinois

List of Pro Bono Legal Service Providers

Updated January 2017

http://www.justice.gov/eoir/list-pro-bono-legal-service-providers

Chicago Immigration Court

Chicago, Illinois

**National Immigrant Justice Center
(A Heartland Alliance Affiliated Partner)***

208 S. LaSalle St., Ste. 1300
Chicago, IL 60604
Tel: (312) 660-1370
Fax: (312) 660-1505
Tel: (312) 263-0901 (Detainees)
Tel: (773) 672-6599 (Family members calling about a detainee)
www.immigrantjustice.org
• Also provides in-court help desk services in the Chicago Court

Marsh Immigrant Law Center NFP*

5433 S East View Park
Chicago, IL 60615
(773) 684-4740
immcl@emarshlaw.com
emarshlaw.com

• By appointment only

Legal Assistance Foundation of Metropolitan Chicago*

120 S. LaSalle Street, Suite 900
Chicago, IL 60603-3425
312-341-1070

List of Pro Bono Legal Service Providers

http://www.justice.gov/eoir/list-pro-bono-legal-service-providers

Louisiana

List of Pro Bono Legal Service Providers

Updated January 2017

http://www.justice.gov/eoir/list-pro-bono-legal-service-providers

New Orleans Immigration Court

New Orleans, Louisiana	
Loyola University New Orleans College of Law* Loyola Law Clinic & Center for Social Justice 7214 St. Charles Ave, Box 902 New Orleans, LA 70118 (504) 861-5590 (504) 861-5440 loyno.edu/lawclinic/ • All cases including asylum	**Catholic Charities of the Diocese** **Of Baton Rouge-Immigration Legal Services*** 1900 S. Acadian Thruway Baton Rouge, LA 70821-4213 Tel: (225) 346-0660
Hispanic Apostolate Immigration Services* 2505 Maine Avenue Metarie, LA 70003 Tel: (504) 457-3462 Fax: (504) 532-6962 hispanicapostolate@ccano.org	**Project Ishmael*** 3401 Canal St New Orleans, LA 70119 Phone: (504) 233-3057 Fax: (504) 515-0315 projectishmaelnola@gmail.com projectishmaelnola.org • Children in the greater New Orleans area only

List of Pro Bono Legal Service Providers

http://www.justice.gov/eoir/list-pro-bono-legal-service-providers

Oakdale Immigration Court

Oakdale, Louisiana	
Catholic Charities Diocese of Baton Rouge* 1900 S. Acadian Thruway Baton Rouge, LA 70808 Tel: (225) 346-0660 Fax: (225) 346-0020	**Loyola University New Orleans College of Law*** Loyola Law Clinic & Center for Social Justice 7214 St. Charles Ave, Box 902 New Orleans, LA 70118 (504) 861-5590 (504) 861-5440 loyno.edu/lawclinic/ • All cases including asylum

Maryland

List of Pro Bono Legal Service Providers

http://www.justice.gov/eoir/list-pro-bono-legal-service-providers

Baltimore Immigration Court

Baltimore, Maryland (page 1 of 3)

Ayuda*

6925 B Willow Street NW
Washington, DC 20012
(202) 387-4848

- By appointment only
- May charge a nominal fee

- No representation of detained non-citizens
- Ayuda Project END: Represents victims of immigration services or notario fraud in DC matters

- Will represent non-citizens in asylum proceedings
- Languages: Spanish, French, and interpretation for other languages as needed

Baltimore Immigration Consult Project*

University of Maryland Francis King Carey School of Law
500 W. Baltimore Street
Baltimore, MD 21201
Tel: (410) 706-3295
Fax: (410) 706-5856
law.umaryland.edu/programs/clinic/initiatives/immigration/
- Will accept limited removal cases
- Pro bono consultations and referral

Capital Area Immigrants' Rights (CAIR) Coalition*

1612 K Street, NW, Ste. 204

Washington, DC 20006
(202) 331-3320 - Main Line
(202) 331-3329 - Detention Hotline
• Fax: (202) 331-3341
Provides legal services to detained individuals at the Arlington and Baltimore Courts

Human Rights First*

805 15th Street NW, Suite 900
Washington DC 20005
Phone: (202) 370-3313
    humanrightsfirst.org/ayslum/asylum-seekers-and-potential-clients
refugee-protection/probono-program/

- Provide representation for non-detained asylum seekers before the Arlington and Baltmore Courts who are admitted into our program
- Must be afraid to return to home country due to persecution or torture

- No walk-ins, call via telephone for assistance
- Leave a message and our staff will call you back to conduct a full interview
- Languages: Spanish, French, Amharic, Tigrinya, others as needed

Kids in Need of Defense (KIND)*
Baltimore Office

1800 N Charles St, Suite 810

Baltimore, MD 21201
Tel: (443) 470-9437
Fax: (410) 837-4776

infobaltimore@supportkind.org
supportkind.org
- KIND only represents minors and unnacompanied children
- KIND ayuda a menores de edad y nino/as no-acompanados

Catholic Immigration Services, Inc.*
1720 Eye Street, NW, Ste. 607
Washington, DC 20006
Tel: (202) 466-6611 or (202) 466-6612
Fax: (202) 466-6633

• Represents aliens in removal proceedings including aliens seeking asylum.

List of Pro Bono Legal Service Providers

http://www.justice.gov/eoir/list-pro-bono-legal-service-providers

Baltimore, Maryland (page 2 of 3)

Georgetown University Law Center
Center for Applied Legal Studies*
600 New Jersey Avenue, NW, Suite 332
Washington, DC 20001
(202) 662-9565
- Call in first. By appointment only.
- Represents aliens in Asylum removal proceedings.
- Represents only non-detainees.

Catholic Charities Immigration Legal Services*
(Baltimore Archdiocese)
430 S. Broadway
Baltimore, MD 21231
(410) 534-8015
- Represents deteined and non-deteainedindividuals
in removal proceedings, including asylum
Consultations to individuals detained on the Eastern
in MD. May charge a nominal fee
- Detainees in Dorchester and Worchester may write
for a consultation

Immigration Legal Services Associated Catholic Charities*

430 S Broadway
Baltimore, MD 21231
(410) 534-8015
(443) 573-6176
ilsinfo@cc-md.org
cc-md.org/esperanza

- Pro bono services for victims of crime and most
unaccompanied minors

- Family and humanitarian based immigration legal
services for nominal fee, with fee waiver available

- Pro bono case placement and mentorship
- Limited detained representation

Catholic Charities Immigration Legal Services*

924 G Street, N.W.
Washington, DC 20001
Walk-in Intake: Tuesdays
Nominal Consultation Fee
9:30am to 11:30am
Questions: (202)772-4352
or
1618 Monroe Street, N.W.
Washington, DC 20010
Walk-in Intake: Wednesdays
Nominal Consultation Fee
9:00am to 1:00pm
Questions: (202) 939-2420
or
201 E. Diamond Avenue, 3rd floor
Gaithersburg, MD 20877

Group talk: Wednesdays, 12:00pm
Nominal Consultation Fee
Questions: 301-740-2523
or
12247 Georgia Avenue
Silver Spring, MD 20902

Walk-in: Thursdays
Nominal Consultation Fee

9:00am to 11:00am

Questions: (301) 942-1790

- First come, first served
- Bring all documents
- If you've been arrested, bring related documents

* Non Profit Organization
** Referral Service
*** Private Attorney

List of Pro Bono Legal Service Providers

Updated January 2017

http://www.justice.gov/eoir/list-pro-bono-legal-service-providers

Baltimore, Maryland (page 3 of 3)	
University of Maryland and World Relief Joint Immigration Clinic* University of Maryland School of Law 500 W. Baltimore Street, Suite 360 Baltimore, MD 21201 (410) 706-3295 http://www.law.umaryland.edu/programs/clinic/initiatives/immigration/ • Provides free one-time consultation with an experienced immigration attorney for individuals in removal proceedings in Maryland. • Consultations are held the 1st and 3rd Friday of ever month. Individuals must arrive between 9:00 and 9:30 a.m. and bring all papers relating to the court and their immigration cases. If the case is based on a marriage, both husband and wife must attend the consultation.	**HIAS (Silver Spring)*** 1300 Spring St, Suite 500 Silver Spring, MD 20190 Phone: (301) 844-7248 legalhelp@hias.org hias.org • Children and families from Central America seeking humanitarian relief • Asylum seekers who are scientists, sholars, artists, or professionals • Languages: Spanish and Portugeuse

Massachusetts

List of Pro Bono Legal Service Providers

http://www.justice.gov/eoir/list-pro-bono-legal-service-providers

Boston Immigration Court

Boston, Massachusetts (page 1 of 2)	
Catholic Charities Refugee and Immigration Services* 275 West Broadway South Boston, MA 02127 Tel: (617) 464-8100 Fax: (617) 464-8150 • Legal Clinic for advice, referral and forms assistance. • Family reunification visas. • Immigrant victims of domestic violence and U Visas. • Special Immigrant Juveniles. • Representation dependent upon income. • Immigrant victims of human trafficking.	**Political Asylum/Immigration Representation Project (PAIR)*** 98 North Washington Street, Suite 106 Boston, MA 02114 Phone: (617) 742-9296 Fax: (617) 742-9385 • Clients must meet income eligibility guidelines • Asylum applicants; Special Immigrant Juveniles and detained on a limited basis; • Phone intake for detainees and families from 1-3pm, M-Th; by appointment only • Know your rights presentations conducted at Suffolk, Bristol County Jail, Plymouth County Correctional Facilities
Community Legal Aid* 405 Main Street, 4th Floor Worcester, MA 01608 Tel: (508) 752-3718 Fax: (508) 752-5918 and One Monarch Place Springfield, MA 01144 Tel: (413) 781-7814 Fax: (413) 746-3221 • Free representation to non-citizens seeking humanitarian immigration relief, including asylum, relief under the Violence Against Women Act, Special Immigrant Juvenile Status, U visas for crime victims, and T visas for trafficking victims. • Services available only to low-income residents of Central and Western Massachusetts (Berkshire, Franklin, Hampden, Hampshire, and Worcester Counties).	**University of Massachusetts School of Law - Dartmouth*** Immigration Law Clinic 333 Faunce Corner Road North Dartmouth, MA 02747 Tel: (508) 985-1174 Fax: (508) 985-1136 • Eligibility is based on income. • Interpreters provided upon request. • Limited representation is available during May – August. • Inquiries are accepted by telephone or mail.

List of Pro Bono Legal Service Providers

http://www.justice.gov/eoir/list-pro-bono-legal-service-providers

Boston, Massachusetts (page 2 of 2)	
Community Legal Services Counseling Center* One West Street Cambridge, MA 02139 Tel: (617) 661-1010 Fax: (617) 661-3289 • Represents aliens in Asylum proceedings and victims of domestic violence seeking lawful permanent residence. • Representation dependent upon income.	**Kids in Need of Defense (KIND)*** Boston Office c/o Nutter McClennen & Fish LLP Seaport West, 155 Seaport Blvd. 5th Floor Boston, MA 02210 Tel: (617) 207-4138 Fax: (617) 336-7438 infoboston@supportkind.org supportkind.org • KIND only represents minors and unnacompanied children • KIND ayuda a menores de edad y nino/as no-acompanados
Immigrant Legal Advocacy Project (ILAP)* 309 Cumberland Ave., Ste 201 P.O. Box 171917 Portland, ME 04112 (207) 780-1593 (800) 497-8505, Toll Free, Maine residents only • Represents aliens in Asylum proceeding. • Representation in removal proceedings before DHS • Immigration Clinic, consultations and referrals, pro se assistance, and full representation. • Representation limited to Maine residents. • Nominal fees apply, depending on income.	

List of Pro Bono Legal Service Providers

http://www.justice.gov/eoir/list-pro-bono-legal-service-providers

Michigan

List of Pro Bono Legal Service Providers

Updated January 2017

http://www.justice.gov/eoir/list-pro-bono-legal-service-providers

Detroit Immigration Court

Detroit, Michigan

University of Detroit Mercy School of Law*

Immigration Law Clinic
651 E. Jefferson
Detroit, MI 48226
(313) 596-0200

List of Pro Bono Legal Service Providers

http://www.justice.gov/eoir/list-pro-bono-legal-service-providers

Minnesota

List of Pro Bono Legal Service Providers

Updated January 2017

http://www.justice.gov/eoir/list-pro-bono-legal-service-providers

Bloomington Immigration Court

Bloomington, Minnesota	
The Advocates for Human Rights* 330 Second Avenue S., Suite 800 Minneapolis, MN 55401 Tel: (612) 341-9845 Fax: (612) 341-2971 email: hrights@advrights.org website: www.theadvocatesforhumanrights.org • Represents Asylum Seekers • Represent individuals in Minnesota, North Dakota & South Dakota	**Immigrant Law Center of Minnesota, Oficina Legal*** 450 North Syndicate, Suite 200 St. Paul, MN 55104 Tel: (651) 641-1011 Fax: (651) 641-1131 oficinalegal@ilcm.org ilcm.org • Represent low-income immigrants of any nationality detained or residing in MN
Civil Society* 332 Minnesota Street, Ste. E-1436 St. Paul, MN 55101 Tel: (651) 291-0713 Fax: (651) 291-2588 website: http://www.civilsocietyhelps.org email: office@civilsocietyhelps.org • Represents all detained and non-detained immigrant victims of crime, regardless of nationality.	

* Non Profit Organization
** Referral Service
*** Private Attorney

List of Pro Bono Legal Service Providers
http://www.justice.gov/eoir/list-pro-bono-legal-service-providers

Updated January 2017

Missouri

List of Pro Bono Legal Service Providers

Updated January 2017

http://www.justice.gov/eoir/list-pro-bono-legal-service-providers

Kansas City Immigration Court

Kansas City and Saint Louis, Missouri	
Kim Allen Murray, Attorney Rebecca Feldman, Attorney **Immigration Law Project*** Legal Services of Eastern Missouri 4232 Forest Park Ave. St. Louis, MO 63108 Tel: (314) 256-8756 Fax: (314) 534-1028 • We only serve people in eastern Missouri.	**Catholic Immigration Law Project *** 100 N. Tucker Blvd., Suite 726 Saint Louis, MO 63101-1915 Tel: (314) 977-7282 Fax: (314) 977-3334 sfcsstl.org • Limited to low-income individuals living in the counties of the Archdiocese of Saint Louis; • Languages: Spanish, Bosnian
Migrant and Immigrant Community Action Project* 1600 South Kingshighway Blvd, Suite 2N St. Louis, MO 63110 Tel: (314) 995-6995 Fax: (314) 735-4359 www.mica-project.org	**The Clinic at Sharma-Crawford Attorneys at Law*** Fax: 816-994-2310 515 Avenida Cesar E. Chavez Kansas City, MO 64108 Tel: 816-994-2300

* Non Profit Organization
** Referral Service
*** Private Attorney

List of Pro Bono Legal Service Providers

Updated January 2017

http://www.justice.gov/eoir/list-pro-bono-legal-service-providers

Nevada

List of Pro Bono Legal Service Providers

Updated January 2017

http://www.justice.gov/eoir/list-pro-bono-legal-service-providers

Las Vegas Immigration Court

Las Vegas, Nevada	
Catholic Charities of Southern Nevada* Immigration Department 1511 N. Las Vegas Blvd. Las Vegas, NV 89101 Tel: (702) 383-8387 Fax: (702) 385-7748 • Charges nominal fee. • Will represent respondents in asylum.	**University of Nevada, Las Vegas** **William S. Boyd School of Law** **Thomas & Mack Legal Clinic*** 4505 S. Maryland Parkway Las Vegas, Nevada 89170 Tel:(702) 895-2080 Fax (702) 895-2081 or Mailing Address PO Box 71075 Las Vegas, NV 89170-1075 • Will represent indigent clients in immigration and asylum proceedings pro bono

List of Pro Bono Legal Service Providers

http://www.justice.gov/eoir/list-pro-bono-legal-service-providers

New Jersey

List of Pro Bono Legal Service Providers

Updated January 2017

http://www.justice.gov/eoir/list-pro-bono-legal-service-providers

Newark and Elizabeth Immigration Courts

Elizabeth and Newark, New Jersey (page 1 of 2)	
African Hispanic Immigration Organization (AHIO), Inc.* 4815 Westfield Ave Pennsauken, New Jersey 08110 (856) 324-5098 and 5 Central Ave. Newark, NJ 07102 Tel: 973-370-0907 Fax: 973-850-0707 Email: ahiolaw@gmail.com Website: www.ahiolaw.org	**The Hebrew Immigrant Aid Society (HIAS)*** HIAS New York Office 411 Fifth Ave. Suite 1006 New York, NY 10016 Tel: (212) 613-1454 or (212) 613-1376 Fax: (212) 967-4443 • Elizabeth, NJ, only • Contacts: Simon Wettenhall /Aleksander Milch • Provides free legal representation for asylum applicants who are: • Scientists, scholars, students, artists or other professionals or, • Detained or paroled survivors of torture.
Legal Services of New Jersey (LSNJ)* 100 Metroplex Drive at Plainfield Avenue Edison, NJ 08818 All callers (non-detained): Office: (888)576-5529 (toll free); (732) 572-9100 Fax: (732) 572-0066 • All detained callers should call LSNJ through the free call-in system provided by ICE • Handoutsare available in the courtrooms and detention facilities	
	Human Rights First* 75 Broad Street, Floor 31 New York, NY 10004 Tel: (212) 845-5200 Detention Hotline: (212) 629-6170 (open 2-5pm Monday – Friday) Fax: (212) 845-5299 • Contacts: Hamon Madi, Jacqueline Rojas, Lamise Abdel Rahman • Represent detained and non-detained individuals seeking asylum before the New York and New Jersey immigration courts
Camden Center for Law and Social Justice, Inc.* 126 N Broadway Camden, NJ 08102 Tel: (856) 583-2950 Fax: (856) 583-2955 info@cclsj.org cclsj.org	
El Centro Hispano Americano* 525 East Front Street Plainfield, NJ 07060 Tel: (908) 753-8730 Fax: (201) 753-8463 • All cases including asylum • May charge a nominal fee	**American Friends Service Committee*** Immigrants Rights Program Director: Amy Gottlieb 89 Market Street, 6th Floor Newark, NJ 07102 Tel: (973) 643-1924 Fax: (973) 643-8924 • All cases including asylum. • May charge a nominal fee.

* Non Profit Organization
** Referral Service
*** Private Attorney

List of Pro Bono Legal Service Providers

Updated January 2017

http://www.justice.gov/eoir/list-pro-bono-legal-service-providers

Elizabeth and Newark, New Jersey (page 2 of 2)	
American Friends Service Committee, Immigrant Rights Program* 89 Market St, 6th floor Newark, NJ 07102 Tel: (9730 643-1924 Fax: (973) 643-8924 afsc.org • Detained and non-detained NJ residents before NJ immigration courts • Phone for Elizabeth Detention Center: (973) 474-9861 • Phone for all other callers: (973) 643-1924 • Languages: English, Spanish, French	**Kids In Need of Defense (KIND)*** Newark Office c/o Lowenstein Sandler LLP 65 Livingston Avenue Roseland, NJ 07068 Tel: (862) 926-2080 Fax: (973) 597-2400 infonewark@supportkind.org supportkind.org • KIND only represents minors and unnacompanied children • KIND ayuda a menores de edad y nino/as no-acompanados

New York

List of Pro Bono Legal Service Providers

Updated January 2017

http://www.justice.gov/eoir/list-pro-bono-legal-service-providers

Buffalo Immigration Court

Buffalo, New York	
Legal Aid Society of Rochester, Inc.* One West Main Street, Rm. 800 Rochester, NY 14614 (585) 295-5745 (within Monroe County) (800) 963-5604 (outside Monroe County) • Represents aliens seeking Asylum • Representation limited to persons residing in Allegany, Cattaraugus, Chautauqua, Genesee, Livingston, Monroe, Niagara, Ontario, Orleans, Seneca, Steuben, Wayne, Wyoming, and Yates Counties • Will not represent detained aliens	**Erie County Bar Association*** Volunteer Lawyers Project 237 Main Street, Suite 1000 Buffalo, NY 14203 (716) 847-0662 ext 301 non-detained & women (716) 847-0752 for men detained at BFDF • Will only represent low-income
Anne E. Doebler, Esq.** 14 Lafayette Square, Suite 1800 Buffalo, NY 14203 Tel: (716) 898-8568 Fax: (716) 898-8929	

List of Pro Bono Legal Service Providers

http://www.justice.gov/eoir/list-pro-bono-legal-service-providers

New York Immigration Court

New York, New York (page 1 of 3)	
Catholic Charities of New York* Catholic Charities Community Services 80 Maiden Lane, 13th Floor New York, NY 10038 (212) 419-3700 • Languages: Spanish, Haitian-Creole, Mandarin, Cantonese, French, Russian, Polish, Albanian, Greek, Macedonian, Serbo-Croatian, Arabic, Turkish, Bosnian, Amharic, Italian, Hindi, Urdu, Punjab, Vietnamese, Portuguese, Thai • Asylum: Yes • May Charge Nominal Fee • Will appear at 26 Federal Plaza Court and Varick St. Court	**Human Rights First*** 75 Broad Street, Floor 31 New York, NY 10004 Tel: (212) 845-5200 Detention Hotline: (212) 629-6170 (open 2-5pm Monday – Friday) Fax: (212) 845-5299 • Detention hotline: (212) 629-6170 (Open 2-5pm, Mon-Fri) • Contacts: Hamon Madi, Jacqueline Rojas, Lamise Abdel Rahman • Represent detained and non-detained individuals seeking asylum before the New York and New Jersey immigration courts
Northern Manhattan Coalition for Immigrant Rights* 665 W. 182nd Street New York, NY 10033 Tel: (212) 781-0648 Fax: (212) 781-0943 Attn: Mayra Angelica Rios • Will appear at 26 Federal Plaza Court and Varick St. Court • No Asylum • Limited to Non-Detained Cases only • Languages: Spanish	**Migration Office of Catholic Charities, Diocese of Rockville Centre*** 143 Shleigel Blvd, Amityville, NY 11701 (631) 789-5210 • Languages: Russian, French, Spanish, Italian, Mandarin • Will appear at 26 Federal Plaza Court and Varick St. Court • Available for VAWA, Cancellation of removal, Asylum, NACARA, TPS, U & T visas • Serves Nassau and Suffolk counties, Long Island
Central American Legal Assistance* 240 Hooper Street Brooklyn, NY 11211 (718) 486-6800 • Language(s): Spanish • Will appear at 26 Federal Plaza Court and Varick St. Court	**Kids In Need of Defense (KIND)*** New York Office 1410 Broadway, Suite 1401 New York, NY 10018 Tel: (646) 677-9900 infonewyork@supportkind.org supportkind.org • KIND only represents minors and unnacompanied children • KIND ayuda a menores de edad y nino/as no-acompanados

List of Pro Bono Legal Service Providers

http://www.justice.gov/eoir/list-pro-bono-legal-service-providers

New York, New York (page 2 of 3)

City Bar Justice Center*

42 West 44th Street
New York, NY 10036
(212) 382-6710 – must call to make appointment; no walk-in service provided
• Language(s): Spanish, French
• Limited to Asylum; and U, T or VAWA relief for survivors of violent crimes including: domestic violence, child abuse, sexual assaults, hate crimes or human trafficking
• Will appear at 26 Federal Plaza Court and Varick St. Court

HIAS*

333 Seventh Ave., 16th Floor
New York, NY 10001-5004

Tel: (212) 613 1454 / (212) 613 1376
Fax: (212) 967 4442
Contacts: Simon Wettenhall /Aleksander Milch
Provides free legal representation for asylum applicants who are:
• Scientists, scholars, students, artists or other professionals or,
• Detained or paroled survivors of torture.

African Hispanic Immigration Organization*

5 Central Ave.
Newark, NJ 07102
Tel: 973-370-0907
Fax: 973-850-0707

Website: www.ahiolaw.org
Email: ahiolaw@gmail.com

Catholic Migration Services*

191 Joralemon Street, 4th Floor

Brooklyn, NY 11201
(718) 236-3000

 And
47-01 Queens Boulevard, Suite 203B
Sunnyside, NY 11104
(347) 472-3500

• Languages: Spanish, Haitian-Creole, Albanian, Arabic, French, Catalan, and Greek.
• ONLY residents of Brooklyn and Queens County
• Represents individuals seeking asylum and all other forms of relief, including VAWA, 212(c), U & T visas, and cancellation of removal
• Will appear at 26 Federal Plaza Court
• We do not charge a fee for our representation

Safe Horizon Immigration Law Project*

50 Court Street, 8th floor
Brooklyn, New York 11201

(718) 943-8632
• Language(s): Spanish, Russian
• Asylum: Yes

• Limited to: Priority for survivors of domestic abuse, persecution, and/or torture
• Can represent those with non-violent criminal offenses
• Will appear at 26 Federal Plaza Court and Varick St. Court

List of Pro Bono Legal Service Providers

Updated January 2017

http://www.justice.gov/eoir/list-pro-bono-legal-service-providers

New York, New York (page 3 of 3)	
The Legal Aid Society Immigration Law Unit* 199 Water Street, 3rd Floor New York, NY 10038-3500 Tel: (212) 577-3300 • Language(s): Russian, French, Spanish, Italian, Mandarin • Detained and non-detained cases before New York City Immigration Courts (except Wackenhut), including with criminal convictions, seeking asylum • Coordinates the Juvenile Immigration Representation Project for persons aged 18 and under in removal proceedings • Immigration Detention Hotline open Wednesdays and Fridays from 1 to 5 p.m. Will accept collect calls from detention facilities at (212) 577-3456. • Will appear at 26 Federal Plaza Court and Varick St. Court	**ILS Immigration Legal Services, Inc.*** Eleanor Lam, Esq. 481 Main Street, Suite 504 New Rochelle, NY 10801 Tel: (888) 631-6686 Fax: (800) 517-6785 Email: info@ilsny.org Web: http://www.ilsny.org • Language(s): Spanish, English • Appointment required • By appointment in: Manhattan, Queens, Bronx, Brooklyn, Long Island, and others • Limited: pro bono gender-based asylum • Will appear at 26 Federal Plaza Court and Varick St. Court

* Non Profit Organization
** Referral Service
*** Private Attorney

List of Pro Bono Legal Service Providers

Updated January 2017

http://www.justice.gov/eoir/list-pro-bono-legal-service-providers

North Carolina

* Non Profit Organization
** Referral Service
*** Private Attorney

List of Pro Bono Legal Service Providers

Updated January 2017

http://www.justice.gov/eoir/list-pro-bono-legal-service-providers

Charlotte Immigration Court

Charlotte, North Carolina	
North Carolina Justice Center* Immigrants Legal Assistance Project P.O. Box 28068 224 S. Dawson St. Raleigh, NC 27611 1-888-251-2776 Attorneys: Kaci Bishop, Lisa Chun, Attracta Kelly • Accept calls from new immigration clients only on Tuesdays • Do not accept walk-in clients • If you are contacting us for the first time, please call on Tuesdays at 1-888-251-2776 between the hours of 9:00 a.m. and 5:00 p.m • Se habla Español. For information regarding the types of cases we handle, please visit our web-site at www.ncjustice.org	

List of Pro Bono Legal Service Providers

http://www.justice.gov/eoir/list-pro-bono-legal-service-providers

Ohio

List of Pro Bono Legal Service Providers

http://www.justice.gov/eoir/list-pro-bono-legal-service-providers

Cleveland Immigration Court

Cleveland, Ohio	
The Legal Aid Society of Cleveland* 1223 West Sixth Street Cleveland, OH 44113 (888) 817-3777 • Individuals eligible for services include low income detained or non-detained individuals • Non-detained individuals must live in Ashtabula, Cuyahoga, Geauga, lake or Loraine counties	**International Institute of Akron*** 207 East Tallmadge Avenue Akron, OH 44310 (330) 376-5106 • Will represent aliens in Asylum proceedings. • May charge nominal fees and are unable to represent detained cases.
• Detained individuals must be detained in either Bedford Heights City Jail or Seneca County Jail, and must have lived in Ashtabula, Cuyahoga, Geauga, Lake or Lorain counties immediately prior to being detained • Will not represent indigent aliens in asylum proceedings • Services are provided in any language	**Cleveland Catholic Charities** **Migration and Refugee Services** **Immigration Legal Services*** 7800 Detroit Avenue Cleveland, OH 44102 Tel: (216) 939-3769 Fax: (216) 939-3890 www.ccdocle.org/migration-and-refugee-services • Will represent indigent clients in asylum proceedings • Will represent individuals before Executive Office for immigration Review, U.S. Citizenship and Immigration Services

* Non Profit Organization
** Referral Service
*** Private Attorney

List of Pro Bono Legal Service Providers

Updated January 2017

http://www.justice.gov/eoir/list-pro-bono-legal-service-providers

Oregon

List of Pro Bono Legal Service Providers

Updated January 2017

http://www.justice.gov/eoir/list-pro-bono-legal-service-providers

Portland Immigration Court

Portland, Oregon	
Immigration Counseling Service (ICS)*	**Lutheran Community Service of NW***
519 S.W. Park Ave, Ste. 610	605 SE Cesar E. Chavez Blvd.
Portland, Oregon 97205	Portland, Oregon 97214
Tel: (503) 221-1689	Tel: (503) 731-9538
(503) 221-3063	Fax: (503) 233-0667
ics-law.org	http://www.lcsnw.org/
• Languages: Spanish	• Referral services available.

* Non Profit Organization
** Referral Service
*** Private Attorney

List of Pro Bono Legal Service Providers

Updated January 2017

http://www.justice.gov/eoir/list-pro-bono-legal-service-providers

Pennsylvania

List of Pro Bono Legal Service Providers

Updated January 2017

http://www.justice.gov/eoir/list-pro-bono-legal-service-providers

Philadelphia Immigration Court

Philadelphia, Pennsylvania	
Camden Center for Law and Social Justice, Inc.* Immigration Service Office 126 Broadway Camden, NJ 08102 Tel: (856) 583-2950 Fax: (856) 583-2955 or 15 North California Avenue Atlantic City, NJ (609) 348-2111	**Prime - Ecumenical Commitment to Refugees*** 129 Owen Ave., P.O. Box 5 Lansdowne, PA 19050-0005 Tel: (610) 259-4500 Fax: (610) 259-4515 and 604 New Holland Ave., Suite G Lancaster, PA 17602 Tel: (717) 396-9300 Fax: (717) 396-9374
Catholic Social Services* Archdiocese of Philadelphia 227 N. 18th Street Philadelphia, PA 19103 (215) 854-7019 • No criminal cases. • Will take Asylum cases. • May charge a nominal fee.	**Nationalities Service Center Migration Services*** 1216 Arch St., 4th Floor Philadelphia, PA 19107 (215) 893-8400 (215) 735-4064, fax • May charge a nominal fee. • Will take Asylum cases. • No employment-based cases. • Will accept criminal cases.
African Hispanic Immigration Organization (AHIO), Inc.* 4815 Westfield Avenue Pennsauken, NJ 08110 (856) 324-5098 www.ahiolaw.org	
HIAS Pennsylvania* 2100 Arch Street, 3rd floor Philadelphia, PA 19103 Tel: (215) 832-0900 Fax: (215) 832-0919 hiaspa.org • By appointment only • Intake hours: Tuesday 2-4:30 • Wednesday 9:30-12:30 • Priorities include asylum, youth, interpersonal violence, naturalization and family petitions	

List of Pro Bono Legal Service Providers

Updated January 2017

http://www.justice.gov/eoir/list-pro-bono-legal-service-providers

York Immigration Court

York, Pennsylvania

HIAS and Counsel Migration Services*

2100 Arch Street, 3rd Floor
Philadelphia, PA 19103
(215) 832-0900
• Will represent aliens seeking asylum.
• May charge a nominal fee.
• Representation limited to residents of Southeast
Pennsylvania and Delaware.

Prime - Ecumenical Commitment to Refugees*

129 Owen Ave., P.O. Box 5
Lansdowne, PA 19050-0005
Tel: (610) 259-4500
(610) 259-4515
        and
701 N. Lime St.
Lancaster, PA 17602
Tel: (717) 396-9300
Fax: (717) 396-9374

HIAS (Silver Spring)

1300 Spring St, Suite 500
Silver Spring, MD 20190
Phone: (301) 844-7248
legalhelp@hias.org
hias.org
• Children and families from Central America seeking
humanitarian relief
• Asylum seekers who are scientists, sholars, artists, or
professionals
• Languages: Spanish and Portugeuse

Pennsylvania Immigration Resource Center (PIRC)*

112 Pleasant Acres Rd, PO Box 20339, Suite I
York, PA 17402
Tel: (717) 600-8099
Fax: (717) 600-8044
info@pirclaw
pirclaw.org

• All removal defense work
• Languages: Spanish

Nationalities Service Center*

1300 Spruce Street
Philadelphia, PA 19107
(215) 893-8400
• Will represent aliens seeking asylum.
• May charge a nominal fee.

* Non Profit Organization
** Referral Service
*** Private Attorney

List of Pro Bono Legal Service Providers

Updated January 2017

http://www.justice.gov/eoir/list-pro-bono-legal-service-providers

Tennessee

List of Pro Bono Legal Service Providers

Updated January 2017

http://www.justice.gov/eoir/list-pro-bono-legal-service-providers

Memphis Immigration Court

Memphis, Tennessee	
Community Legal Center* 910 Vance Avenue Memphis, TN 38126 Tel: (901) 543-3395 Fax: (901) 543-0907	**Mid-South Immigration Advocates, Inc.*** 258 North Merton St Memphis, TN 38112 English: (901) 244-4367
Volunteer Immigrant Defense Advocates (VIDA)* 2108 Keller Bend Rd Knoxville, TN 37922 Phone: (895) 410-8432 Fax: (888) 410-9674 info@vidaimmigration.org vidaimmigration.org • Only individuals in East Tennessee • Adults and children • Languages: Spanish	Spanish: (901) 466-8819 info@miamemphis.org www.miamemphis.org • Priority to children's and asylum cases
	Derechos Programa de Inmigracion* Latino Memphis, Inc. 6041 Mt Moriah Ext., Suite 16 Memphis, TN 38115 Hablamos Espanol (901) 410-0195 (904) 609-7028 derechos@latinomemphis.org latinomemphis.org • Will represent foreign national residing in TN, AR, KT, and Northern MS • Provide Pro bono represenation based on household income

List of Pro Bono Legal Service Providers

http://www.justice.gov/eoir/list-pro-bono-legal-service-providers

Texas

List of Pro Bono Legal Service Providers

Updated January 2017

http://www.justice.gov/eoir/list-pro-bono-legal-service-providers

Dallas Immigration Court

Dallas, Texas	
Catholic Charities of Dallas, Inc.* 9461 LBJ Freeway, Suite 100 Dallas, TX 75243 (214) 634-7182 • Representation in removal proceedings for detained and non-detained cases within Dallas area • Will represent aliens in Asylum cases • Does not provide representation for aliens detained at the Big Spring facility, Eden, or Oklahoma	**Baptist Immigration Center*** Alex Camacho, Accredited 507 Titus Street Mckinney, TX 75069 (972) 562-4561 • Do not take cases related to or caused by drug or child abuse • Provide assistance in some cancellation of removal cases
Human Rights Initiative of North Texas, Inc.* 2801 Swiss Avenue Dallas, TX 75204 (214) 855-0520 • Will only represent aliens in the Dallas Immigration Court • Will represent aliens in asylum cases • Will represent juveniles • Will NOT provide representation in detention facilities	

List of Pro Bono Legal Service Providers

Updated January 2017

http://www.justice.gov/eoir/list-pro-bono-legal-service-providers

El Paso Immigration Court

El Paso, Texas	
United Neighborhood Organization (UNO)*	**New Mexico Immigrant Law Center ***
	714 4th Street SW
8660 Montana, Ste. I	Albuquerque, NM 87102
El Paso, TX 79925	(505) 247-1023
(915) 775-1161	nmilc.org
• Will not represent aliens in asylum or refugee cases	• Non-detained only
• May charge a nominal fee	• Specializes in humanitarian remedies
UNO branch location:	**Catholic Charities of Southern New Mexico***
747 E. San Antonio Avenue, Suite 100	
El Paso, TX 79901	2215 South Main St, Suite B
(915) 351-0099	Las Cruces, NM 88005
• Will not represent aliens in asylum or refugee cases.	Tel: (575) 526-9621
• May charge a nominal fee.	Fax: (575) 562-9626
Diocesan Migrant and Refugee Services*	ccdlc@catholiccharitiesdlc.org
	www.catholiccharitiesdlc.org
2400 E. Yandell, Ste. A	
El Paso, TX 79903-3617	
(915) 532-3975	
(915) 532-4071	
info@dmrs-ep.org	
dmrs-ep.org	

List of Pro Bono Legal Service Providers

http://www.justice.gov/eoir/list-pro-bono-legal-service-providers

Harlingen & Port Isabel Immigration Courts

Harlingen, Texas	
Probar - South Texas Pro Bono Asylum Representation* 222 East Van Buren Ave., Suite 300 Harlingen, TX 78550 (956) 425-9231 If calling from the Port Isabel Detention Center, for free call without calling card: • Detainee picks up the phone in the dorm • Presses 1 for English, 2 for Spanish • Enters PIN number • Selects prompt 6 • Enters 5708# (#sign) Will represent aliens in Asylum hearings	**South Texas Immigration Council*** Casa Mexico Bldg. 4793 West Expressway 83 Harlingen, TX 78552 Phone: (956) 425-6987 Fax: (956) 425-7434 • All types of cases • Languages: Spanish
South Texas Immigration Council* 4 E. Levee St. Brownsville, TX 78520 (956) 542-1991 • Will represent aliens in Asylum hearings	**South Texas Immigration Council, Inc.*** 1201 Galveston St. McAllen, TX 78501 (956) 682-5397 Fax: (956) 682-8133 • Will represent aliens in Asylum hearings • May charge a nominal fee
Texas RioGrande Legal Aid, Inc.* 316 S. Closner Blvd. Edinburg, TX 78539 Local Tel: (956) 393-6200 Toll Free Intake: 1-888-988-9996 • Will represent Legal Permanent Residents, United States citizens, and VAWA, U-visa or T-visa applicants	

List of Pro Bono Legal Service Providers

Updated January 2017

http://www.justice.gov/eoir/list-pro-bono-legal-service-providers

Houston Immigration Court

Houston, Texas	
Catholic Charities of the Archdiocese of Galveston-Houston* Cabrini Center for Immigration Legal Assistance 2900 Louisiana St Houston, TX 77006 Tel: (713) 595-4100 Fax: (713) 595-4198 ucreferrals@catholiccharities.org catholiccharities.org • Will represent persons in asylum cases • Childrens cases • Languages: Spanish	**Kids In Need of Defense (KIND)*** Houston Office c/o South Texas College Law 1303 San Jacinto Street, 9th Floor Houston, TX 77002 Tel: 832-779-4030 Fax: (281) 940-2098 infohouston@supportkind.org supportkind.org • KIND only represents minors and unnacompanied children • KIND ayuda a menores de edad y nino/as no-acompanados
Human Rights First* 1303 San Jacinto Street, 9th Floor Houston, TX 77002 (713) 955-1360 • Represent indigent individuals seeking asylum • No walk-ins, call and leave a message • Languages: Spanish, others as needed	**YMCA International Services*** 6300 West Park, Ste. 600 Houston, TX 77057 Tel: (713) 339-9015 Fax: (713) 339-1159 ymcahouston.org/ymca-international/ • Adjustment of status, asylum, appeals, cancellation • Citizenship, detained, family cases, refugee issues • T and U Visas, VAWA, Waivers and Withholding of removal • Languages: Staff speaks over 25 languages

* Non Profit Organization
** Referral Service
*** Private Attorney

List of Pro Bono Legal Service Providers

Updated January 2017

http://www.justice.gov/eoir/list-pro-bono-legal-service-providers

Pearsall Immigration Court

Pearsall, Texas	
American Gateways*	**St. Mary's Immigration and Human Rights Clinic***
One Highland Center	
314 Highland Mall Blvd., Ste. 501	2507 NW 36th St
Austin, TX 78752	San Antonio, TX 78228
(512) 478-0546	Phone: (210) 431-2596
www.americangateways.org	Fax: (210) 431-5700

* Non Profit Organization
** Referral Service
*** Private Attorney

List of Pro Bono Legal Service Providers

Updated January 2017

http://www.justice.gov/eoir/list-pro-bono-legal-service-providers

San Antonio Immigration Court

San Antonio, Texas

American Gateways*

One Highland Center
314 Highland Mall Blvd., Ste. 501
Austin, TX 78752
(512) 478-0546
www.americangateways.org

Catholic Charities Archdiocese of San Antonio, Inc.*

202 W French Place
San Antonio, TX 78212
(210) 433-3256

• Only represents clients in San Antonio Immigration Court

Immigration Clinic of the University of Texas School of Law*

727 East Dean Keeton Street
Austin, TX 78705-3299
(512) 232-1292
• Will represent aliens in Asylum cases
• Clinic is closed from May 1st until September 1st

Refugee & Immigrant Center for Education and Legal Services*

1305 N. Flores
San Antonio, TX 78212
(210) 226-7722
• Will represent aliens in asylum cases

Texas RioGrande Legal Aid, Inc.*

1111 N. Main Ave.
San Antonio, TX 78212
(210) 212-3783
Toll Free: (888) 988-9996
• Will represent Legal Permanent Residents, US citizens, and U-visa or T-visa applicants

St. Mary's Immigration and Human Rights Clinic*

2507 NW 36th St
San Antonio, TX 78228
Phone: (210) 431-2596
Fax: (210) 431-5700

List of Pro Bono Legal Service Providers

http://www.justice.gov/eoir/list-pro-bono-legal-service-providers

Utah

List of Pro Bono Legal Service Providers

http://www.justice.gov/eoir/list-pro-bono-legal-service-providers

Salt Lake City Immigration Court

Salt Lake City, Utah

Utah Pro Bono Asylum Project, c/o Holy Cross Ministries **

860 E 4500 S, Suite 204
Salt Lake City, UT 84107
Tel: (801) 261-3496
Fax: (801) 261-3490
www.holycrossministries.org
• Pro bono referral service for non-detained arriving aliens seeking asylum

* Non Profit Organization
** Referral Service
*** Private Attorney

List of Pro Bono Legal Service Providers

Updated January 2017

http://www.justice.gov/eoir/list-pro-bono-legal-service-providers

Virginia

List of Pro Bono Legal Service Providers

Updated January 2017

http://www.justice.gov/eoir/list-pro-bono-legal-service-providers

Arlington Immigration Court

Arlington, Virginia (page 1 of 2)	
Catholic Charities Immigration Legal Services* 924 G Street, N.W. Washington, DC 20001 Walk-in Intake: Tuesdays Nominal Consultation Fee 9:30am to 11:30am Questions: (202)772-4352 or 1618 Monroe Street, N.W. Washington, DC 20010 Walk-in Intake: Wednesdays Nominal Consultation Fee 9:00am to 1:00pm Questions: (202) 939-2420 or 201 E. Diamond Avenue, 3rd floor Gaithersburg, MD 20877 Group talk: Wednesdays, 12:00pm Questions: 301-740-2523 or 12247 Georgia Avenue Silver Spring, MD 20902 Walk-in: Thursdays Nominal Consultation Fee 9:00am to 11:00am Questions: (301) 942-1790 • First-come, first-served basis. • Please bring all documents related to your immigration case with you. • If you have been arrested, you must bring documents to show the disposition of the case.	**George Washington University Law School Immigration Clinic*** 565 20th St NW Washington, DC 20052 (202) 994-7463 law.gwu.edu/immigration-clinic • All forms of relief from removal • Must call for appointment • Intake is open during academic semesters only
	Human Rights First* 805 15th Street NW, Suite 900 Washington DC 20005 Phone: (202) 370-3313 humanrightsfirst.org/ayslum/asylum-seekers-and-potential-clients refugee-protection/probono-program/ • Provide representation for non-detained asylum seekers before the Arlington and Baltmore Courts who are admitted into our program • Must be afraid to return to home country due to persecution or torture • No walk-ins, call via telephone for assistance • Leave a message and our staff will call you back to conduct a full interview • Languages: Spanish, French, Amharic, Tigrinya, others as needed

List of Pro Bono Legal Service Providers

http://www.justice.gov/eoir/list-pro-bono-legal-service-providers

Arlington, Virginia (page 2 of 2)

Capital Area Immigrants' Rights (CAIR) Coalition*

1612 K Street, NW, Ste. 204
Washington, DC 20006
(202) 331-3320 - Main Line
(202) 331-3329 - Detention Hotline
Fax: (202) 331-3341

• Provides legal services to detained individuals before the Arlington and Baltimore Immigration Courts

Georgetown University Law Center*

Center for Applied Legal Studies
600 New Jersey Avenue, NW, Suite 332
Washington, DC 20001
(202) 662-9565
• Call first. Must have an appointment.
• Represents only non-detainees
• Represents aliens seeking Asylum in removal proceedings

Catholic Immigration Services*

1720 Eye Street, NW, Ste. 607
Washington, DC 20006
(202) 466-6611 or (202) 466-6612
(202) 466-6633, Fax
• Will represent aliens in Asylum proceedings

HIAS (Silver Spring)

1300 Spring St, Suite 500
Silver Spring, MD 20190
Phone: (301) 844-7248
legalhelp@hias.org
hias.org
humanitarian relief
• Asylum seekers who are scientists, sholars, artists, or professionals
• Languages: Spanish and Portugeuse

Kids In Need of Defense (KIND)*

Washington DC Office

2815 Hartland Rd, Suite 110
Falls Church, VA 22043
Tel: (202) 670-3585
Fax: (703) 942-6798
infodc@supportkind.org
supportkind.org

• KIND only represents minors and unnacompanied children
• KIND ayuda a menores de edad y nino/as no-acompanados

Ayuda*

Virginia Office (for Virginia Residents)
2755 Hartland Road, Suite 100
Falls Church, Virginia 22043

(703) 444-7009
DC Office (for DC and Maryland Residents)
6925 B Willow Street NW
Washington, DC 20012
(202) 387-4848
• By appointment only
• No representation of detained non-citizens

• Will represent non-citizens in asylum proceedings
• Languages: Spanish, French, and interpretation for other languages as needed
• Represents victims of immigration services or notario fraud in DC matters

Northern Virginia Family Service*

6400 Arlington Blvd, Suite 100
Falls Church, VA 22042
Fax: (703) 237-2083
nvfs.org

• No detained clients
• Languages: Spanish with interpretation in other languages

Washington

List of Pro Bono Legal Service Providers

http://www.justice.gov/eoir/list-pro-bono-legal-service-providers

Seattle Immigration Court

Seattle, Washington	
Northwest Immigrant Rights Project - Western Washington Office* 615 Second Avenue, Suite 400 Seattle, WA 98104 Phone: (206) 587-4009 Fax: (206) 587-4025 www.nwirp.org • All forms of relief • All forms of relief for detained immigrants	**Northwest Immigrant Rights Project - Granger Office*** 121 Sunnyside Avenue, P.O. Box 270 Granger, WA 98932 Phone: (509) 854-2100 Fax: (509) 854-1500 www.nwirp.org • Only serves those detained at Northwest Detention Center
Northwest Immigrant Rights Project - Wenatchee Office* 37 South Wenatchee Avenue, Suite C Wenatchee, WA 98801 Phone: (509) 570-0054 Fax: (509) 765-9714	• Toll free: (877) 814-6444 (to make free calls from Northwest Detention Center, enter #2279 after PIN) • Languages: Spanish • Leave message with name and A# • Provide group orientations, individual orientations, workshops, and possible referrals to pro bono attorneys
Kids in Need of Defense (KIND)* Seattle Office 1201 Third Ave, Suite 4900 Seattle, WA 98101 (206) 359-3266 (206) 447-1541 infoseattle@supportkind.org supportkind.org • KIND only represents minors and unnacompanied children • KIND ayuda a menores de edad y nino/as no-acompanados	

List of Pro Bono Legal Service Providers

http://www.justice.gov/eoir/list-pro-bono-legal-service-providers

Tacoma Immigration Court

Tacoma, Washington	
Northwest Immigrant Rights Project - Tacoma Office* 402 Tacoma Avenue South, Suite 300 Tacoma, WA 98402 Phone: 253) 383-0519 Fax: (253) 383-0111 www.nwirp.org • Only serves those detained at Northwest Detention Center • Toll free: (877) 814-6444 (to make free calls from Northwest Detention Center, enter #2279 after PIN) • Leave message with name and A# • Provide group orientations, individual orientations, workshops, and possible referrals to pro bono attorneys • Languages: Spanish	**Northwest Immigrant Rights Project - Granger Office*** 121 Sunnyside Avenue, P.O. Box 270 Granger, WA 98932 Phone: (509) 854-2100 Fax: (509) 854-1500 www.nwirp.org • Only serves those detained at Northwest Detention Center • Toll free: (877) 814-6444 (to make free calls from Northwest Detention Center, enter #2279 after PIN) • Leave message with name and A# • Provide group orientations, individual orientations, workshops, and possible referrals to pro bono attorneys • Languages: Spanish
Northwest Immigrant Rights Project - Western Washington Office* 615 Second Avenue, Suite 400 Seattle, WA 98104 Phone: (206) 587-4009 Fax: (206) 587-4025 www.nwirp.org • All forms of relief • All forms of relief for detained immigrants